I0820281

GOVERNOR HOLCOMB

GOVERNOR HOLCOMB

Scenes I'll Forever Hold Dear

PURDUE UNIVERSITY PRESS, WEST LAFAYETTE, INDIANA

I dedicate this album of generosity to the heart of Indiana—the Hoosiers pictured and those not—who build, believe, and breathe life into the very spirit of our great state. After all, it's their dedication to community, their unwavering support for one another, and their unique blend of grit and grace that defines our standing—year after year making Indiana such a special place. The following pages highlight just a snapshot of the architects of our state's rich, modern history, the guardians of our traditions, and the citizens who propel us onward and upward.

Printed in the United States of America.

Cataloging-in-Publication data is on file at the Library of Congress.

978-1-62671-183-9 (hardcover)
978-1-62671-184-6 (epdf)

CONTENTS

PREFACE

As time goes by, I find myself looking back on my tenure as governor of Indiana and am filled with immense pride. I couldn't be more grateful to each team member who devoted their talents to bettering our great state.

Over the course of my two terms, our administration focused on five pillars to guide our work: cultivating a strong and diverse economy, fostering vibrant communities, advancing education, improving health, and delivering good government service. These priorities served as the foundation and focus of everything we accomplished.

It is my hope that this collection of memories will serve as a visual reflection, marking certain highlights along our journey. From unprecedented economic growth and infrastructure investment to advancements in public health and education, each image captures the milestones that moved Indiana forward. Our daily commitment was not only about responding to the current issues of the day, but also about strategically laying the groundwork for a brighter, more prosperous long-term future.

Indiana's success has always been a testament to the power of collaboration and aligned purpose, and I am pleased to share a number of examples for your review.

(Left) Governor-Elect Eric Holcomb, joined by IEDC's Victor Smith, future Secretary of Commerce Jim Schellinger, and Director for Indiana State Government in the UK and Ireland Stephen Bridges, meets with then Rolls-Royce Group President Colin Smith and senior executives on Dec. 5, 2016, during an economic development trip to Derby, United Kingdom.

"Take Indiana to the world,

and bring the world back to Indiana."

–Governor Eric J. Holcomb

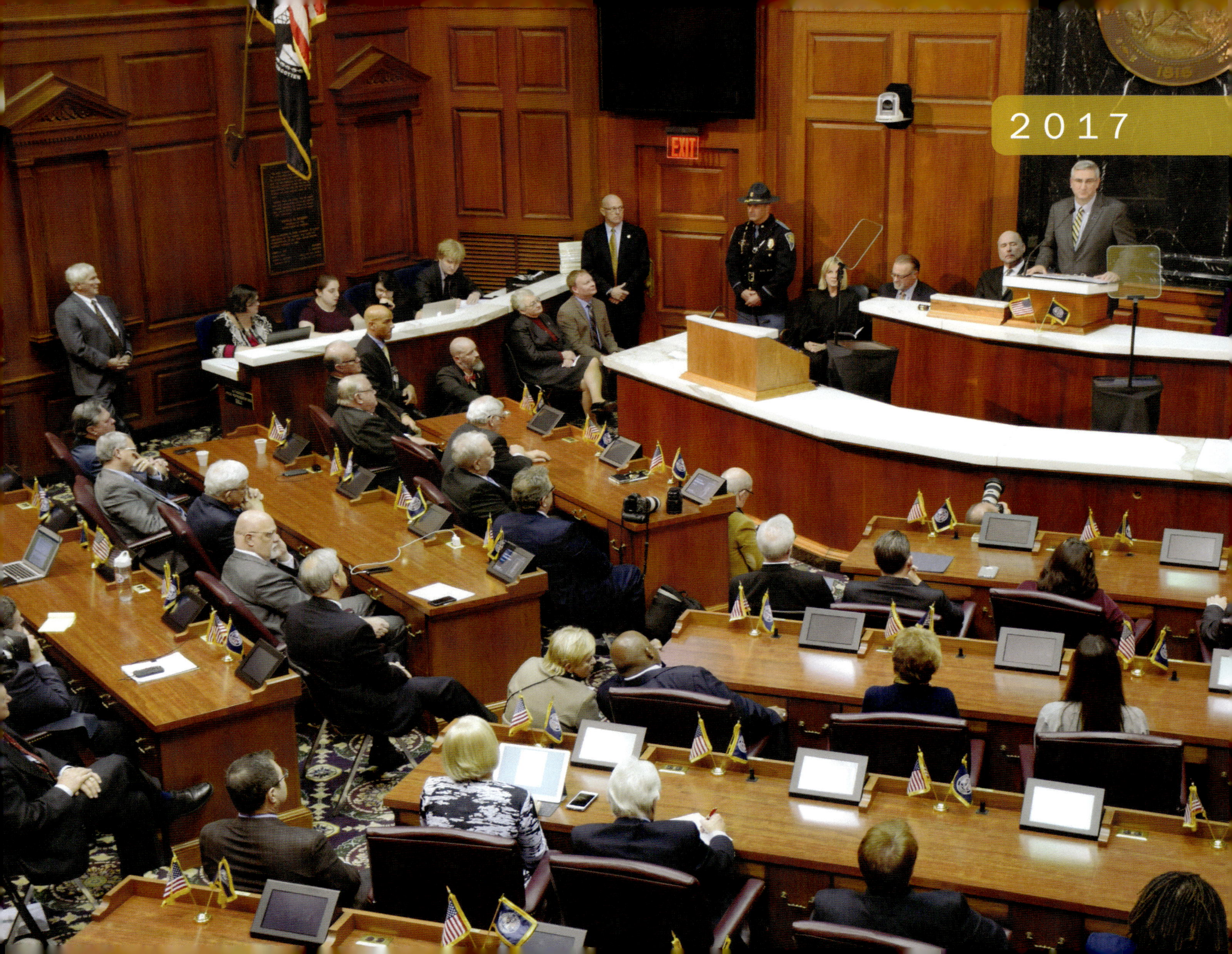

2017

Deputy General Counsel Cindy Carasco and General Counsel Joe Heerens organize executive orders for Gov. Holcomb to sign on Jan. 9, 2017, in the Governor's Office.

(Previous page) Gov. Holcomb delivers his first State of the State Address on Jan. 17, 2017, in the House of Representatives Chamber.

(Above) Gov. Holcomb takes a selfie with students on Jan. 12, 2017, during a Martin Luther King Jr. Day celebration in the Statehouse.

(Facing page) Indiana Supreme Court Chief Justice Loretta Rush swears Gov. Holcomb into office on Jan. 5, 2017, in the Statehouse.

Lt Gov

The 51st Governor of Indiana Eric Holcomb with the 50th Governor of Indiana and 48th Vice President of the United States Mike Pence, the 49th Governor of Indiana Mitch Daniels, and the 46th Governor of Indiana Evan Bayh on Jan. 20, 2017, just before Gov. Holcomb's inauguration ceremony.

Gov. Holcomb is sworn in by Indiana Supreme Court Chief Justice Loretta Rush on Jan. 20, 2017, while First Lady Janet Holcomb holds the 23rd President Benjamin Harrison's personal Bible.

Gov. Holcomb with Toyota Indiana Plant Manager Millie Marshall on Jan. 24, 2017, during a jobs announcement in Princeton.

Gov. Holcomb watches as a Jay County High School student demonstrates a step in the jersey-making process on Feb. 10, 2017, in Portland.

Gov. Holcomb outside Cindy's Diner on Feb. 13, 2017, in Fort Wayne.

Gov. Holcomb watches First Lady Janet Holcomb fire the initial round at the grand opening for the Deer Creek Shooting Range near Cloverdale on her birthday, Feb. 16, 2017.

Gov. Holcomb walks in the Rushville St. Patrick's Day parade on March 11, 2017, in Rushville.

First Lady Janet Holcomb and Gov. Holcomb attend an Army Reserve dinner on March 11, 2017, in Columbus.

Gov. Holcomb offers high fives to a long line of children on March 16, 2017, at the Jewish Community Center in Indianapolis.

Voice of the Indianapolis Indians Howard Kellman and Gov. Holcomb call the Opening Day game on April 6, 2017, at Victory Field in Indianapolis.

Department of Workforce Development Commissioner Steve Braun and Gov. Holcomb with JAG students on March 17, 2017, during their career development conference at Ivy Tech Community College in Indianapolis.

Gov. Holcomb, Indiana State Health Commissioner Jerome Adams, Lt. Gov. Crouch, and legislators celebrate the governor's signing of HEA 1278 on April 10, 2017. The bill assisted with decreasing cervical cancer mortality in Indiana.

Gov. Holcomb with new recipients of the Sagamore of the Wabash award Tom Jernstedt, Muffet McGraw, and George McGinnis on April 17, 2017, in the Governor's Office.

Gov. Holcomb takes a break before an event on April 1, 2017, in Borden.

2017 3A IHSAA Boys Basketball State Champion Zac Owens and Head Coach Chris Hawkins of Crispus Attucks High School talk to Gov. Holcomb on April 10, 2017, in the Governor's Office.

Holocaust survivor and 2017 Sachem Eva Kor and Gov. Eric Holcomb pose with the Sachem Award on April 13, 2017, during a ceremony at the Indiana War Memorial.

Gov. Holcomb, Indiana War Memorial Executive Director J. Stewart Goodwin, and others on May 15, 2017, looking at Gov. Holcomb's brick being added to the Soldiers and Sailors Monument perimeter.

Gov. Holcomb heads down the locker room stairs on May 11, 2017, inside Notre Dame Stadium in South Bend.

Gov. Holcomb, First Lady Janet Holcomb, and First Dog Henry greet Hoosiers on July 15, 2017, at Freudenfest in Oldenburg.

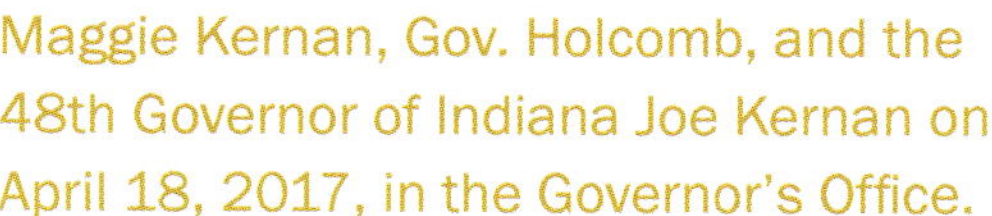

Maggie Kernan, Gov. Holcomb, and the 48th Governor of Indiana Joe Kernan on April 18, 2017, in the Governor's Office.

Gov. Holcomb picks up pizza for his staff on the last day of the Indiana legislative session on April 21, 2017, at Giorgio's Pizza in Indianapolis.

Gov. Holcomb gives a thumbs-up to a crowd on May 18, 2017, before signing new legislation to provide funding to double-track the South Shore Line between Gary and Michigan City in Michigan City.

Gov. Holcomb enters an event to sign HEA 1200, known as "Kate's Law," which requires off-road vehicle operators under the age of 18 to wear helmets. The event was held on June 5, 2017, at Sharon Elementary School in Newburgh.

Gov. Holcomb with Indiana Commissioner Bureau of Indian Affairs Kenny Eagle on July 10, 2017, in the Governor's Office.

Gov. Holcomb holds a newborn while admiring T. C. Steele's portrait of James Whitcomb Riley on June 6, 2017, in the Governor's Office.

Willie Nelson and Gov. Holcomb meet on June 5, 2017, on Nelson's tour bus in Evansville.

Hungarian Minister of Foreign Affairs and Trade Péter Szijjártó, Gov. Holcomb, and IEDC Secretary Jim Schellinger talk to Hungarian Prime Minister Viktor Orbán on June 14, 2017, in Budapest during an economic development trip.

US Environmental Protection Agency Administrator Scott Pruitt and Gov. Holcomb disembark a helicopter on Aug. 2, 2017. Indiana was a stop on Pruitt's State Action Tour, where he visited the Liberty Coal Mine in Warrick County.

Gov. Holcomb receives a basketball from Indiana Conservation Officers and Road to Redemption Recovery group to signify the beginning of healing and partnership between recovering addicts and law enforcement officers on July 27, 2017, in the Governor's Office.

Gov. Holcomb thanks construction workers in Fort Wayne before kicking off his Next Level Roads program on July 17, 2017. The program is investing approximately $60 billion in Indiana's highways over 20 years.

Owner of North American Fairs Danny Huston and Gov. Holcomb strike up a conversation on Aug. 4, 2017, at the opening day of the Indiana State Fair in Indianapolis.

US Secretary of Agriculture Sonny Perdue and Gov. Holcomb catch up on Aug. 8, 2017, during a visit to the Indiana State Fair in Indianapolis.

First Dog Henry, First Lady Janet Holcomb, and Gov. Holcomb walk to the Government Center Plaza on Aug. 10, 2017, on their way to visit local food trucks.

Gov. Holcomb awards Pike High School graduate and Olympic sprinter Lynna Irby a Sagamore of the Wabash award on July 27, 2017, in the Governor's Office. Irby would go on to win an Olympic Gold Medal as part of the US 4 x 400m relay team in the Tokyo Games.

Gov. Holcomb talks to USS *Indianapolis* survivor Edgar Harrell on July 30, 2017, at a reunion of USS *Indianapolis* crew and family members. The sinking of the ship on July 30, 1945, was the greatest single loss of life at sea in the history of the US Navy.

(Above) Gov. Holcomb participates in a computer coding exercise with students on Dec. 5, 2017, in the Statehouse.

(Left) University of Notre Dame President Rev. John I. Jenkins and Gov. Holcomb walk on Aug. 13, 2017, during Notre Dame's 175th anniversary celebration commemorating Father Sorin and the Holy Cross Brothers' journey from Vincennes to South Bend.

South Bend Mayor Pete Buttigieg and Gov. Holcomb join other city, town, and county officials outlining the amount of funds they will receive on Oct. 5, 2017, to commemorate a Community Crossings event.

(Left) Gov. Holcomb and US Secretary of Housing and Urban Development Dr. Ben Carson shake hands while US Rep. Peter Visclosky, US Sen. Todd Young, US Sen. Joe Donnelly, and Lt. Gov. Suzanne Crouch applaud at a press conference on Aug. 7, 2017. The group met with residents in East Chicago to help families displaced from a lead-contaminated public housing complex.

Gov. Holcomb visits with Duke Energy power plant workers on Aug. 30, 2017, in Owensville.

Gov. Holcomb and Tochigi Prefecture Gov. Tomikazu Fukuda share a laugh on Sept. 9, 2017, during an economic trip to Japan.

Gov. Holcomb tours section 6 of the I-69 project with INDOT officials on Oct. 2, 2017, near Martinsville.

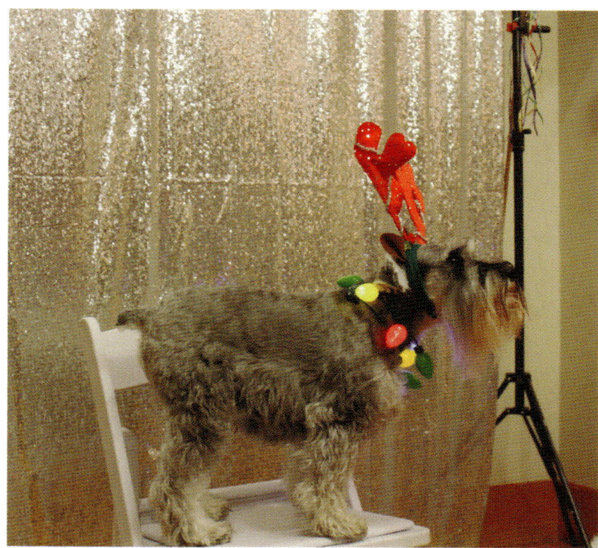

First Dog Henry does his best reindeer impression on Dec. 18, 2017, during a Christmas party at the Governor's Residence.

Gov. Holcomb and Consul General of the US in Mumbai Edgard Kagan tour a Cummins engine plant in Pune, India, on Nov. 1, 2017, during an economic development trip.

Evansville Mayor Lloyd Winnecke and Gov. Holcomb participate in a kickoff on Oct. 26, 2017, to make way for an upgraded terminal at Evansville Regional Airport.

Gov. Holcomb shakes Sen. Rod Bray's hand before delivering his State of the State address on Jan. 9, 2018, in the House of Representatives Chamber.

Gov. Holcomb with House Speaker Brian Bosma and Sen. David Long during a weekly leadership meeting on Feb. 7, 2018, in the Governor's Office.

Gov. Holcomb, US Secretary of Health and Human Services Alex Azar, and FSSA Secretary Dr. Jennifer Walthall announce the extension of the Healthy Indiana plan at a joint press conference on Feb. 2, 2018, in Indianapolis.

Gov. Holcomb and First Lady Janet Holcomb walk with US Sen. Joe Donnelly and others during the Martin Luther King Jr. 50th anniversary celebration on Jan. 12, 2018, in Indianapolis.

Gov. Holcomb unveils a sign touting new nonstop flights from South Bend International Airport to Dallas/Fort Worth and Charlotte on Jan. 18, 2018, in South Bend.

Gov. Holcomb acknowledges a passerby as he walks into The Angler tackle and hunting shop in Jan. 2018 in Hudson.

Gov. Holcomb meets students during manufacturing night at Logansport High School on Jan. 26, 2018.

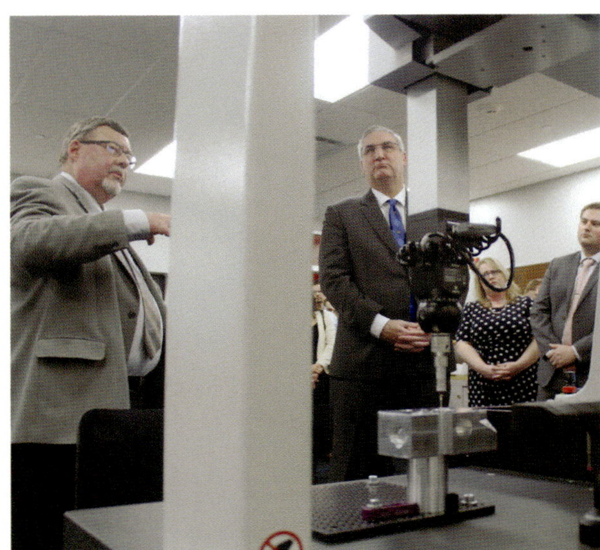

Gov. Holcomb and Lebanon Mayor Matt Gentry tour a Haas manufacturing facility on Feb. 15, 2018, in Lebanon.

Gov. Holcomb looks at the Borg-Warner Trophy while sitting on stage with IndyCar CEO Mark Miles, IMS President Doug Boles, and 2017 Indy 500 Winner Takuma Sato at the ticket unveiling for the 2018 Indy 500 on Feb. 22, 2018, in the Statehouse.

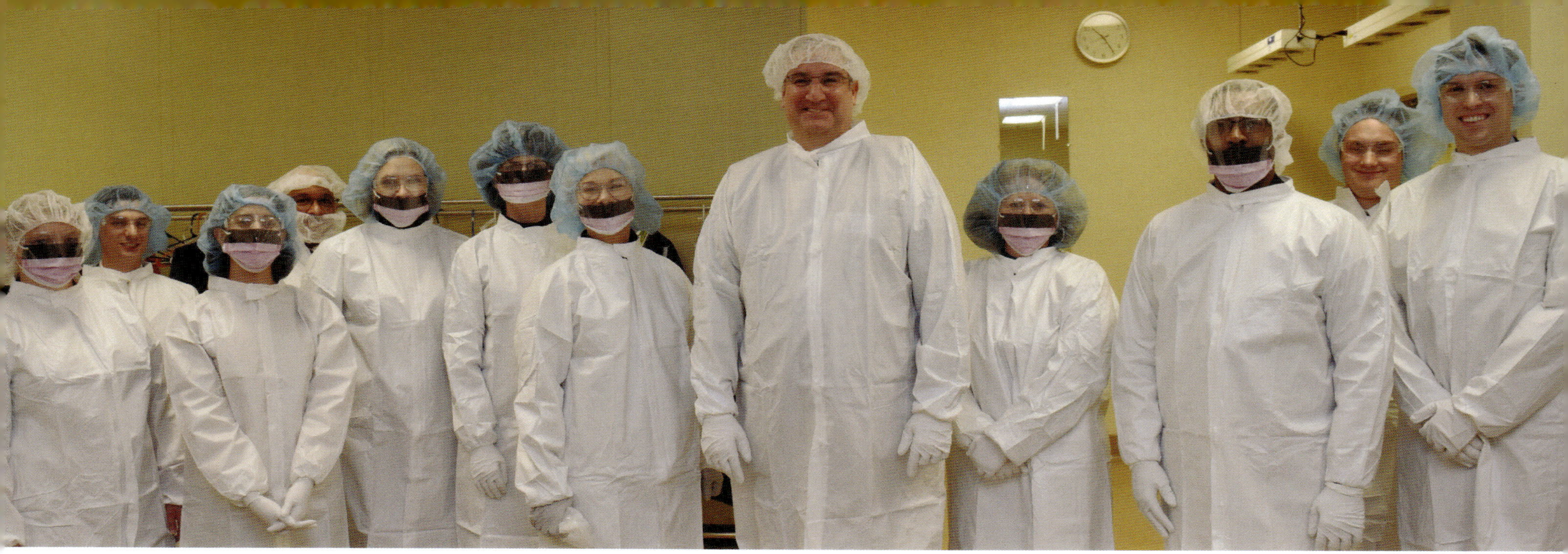

(Above) Gov. Holcomb with Cook Medical employees on March 2, 2018, in Bloomington.

(Right) Gov. Holcomb surveys flood damage in southern Indiana on Feb. 26, 2018, near Madison.

(Far right) Gov. Holcomb browses the beer selection at Goose the Market on March 4, 2018, in Indianapolis. Holcomb made the first Sunday beer purchase after the State's ban on Sunday alcohol sales ended by law.

(Far left) Gov. Holcomb places an order at the counter of Triple XXX in West Lafayette on March 23, 2018.

(Left) 2018 Sachem and Medal of Honor Recipient Sammy Davis with Gov. Holcomb after the Sachem ceremony in the Indiana War Memorial on March 12, 2018, in Indianapolis.

(Below) Gov. Holcomb gives a signing pen to Rep. Kirchhofer during the signing of SEA 360 on March 8, 2018, at Peyton Manning Children's Hospital in Indianapolis. The law aims to improve birthing outcomes.

Gov. Holcomb shoots hoops on a ship during an economic development trip on March 28, 2018, in Canada.

Students at Cumberland Elementary wave lights emulating fireflies before the signing of SEA 236, which made the Say's Firefly the Indiana State Insect on March 23, 2018, in West Lafayette.

DemandJump CEO Christopher Day looks on as Rep. Todd Huston, Gov. Holcomb, and Rep. Timothy Brown sign SEA 257 into law on March 23, 2018, in Indianapolis. The law exempts software as a service from sales tax.

(Right) Gov. Holcomb celebrates the Indiana University Women's Basketball team's NIT Championship game on March 31, 2018, in Bloomington.

(Far right) Gov. Holcomb and University of Notre Dame President Rev. John I. Jenkins celebrate the Notre Dame Women's Basketball team's NCAA National Championship victory on April 2, 2018, in Columbus, OH.

(Facing page) Gov. Holcomb meets with Canadian Prime Minister Justin Trudeau during an economic development trip on March 26, 2018, in Ottowa, Canada.

(Above) Gov. Holcomb announces Infosys will establish a US Education Center in Indianapolis to train its US workers on April 26, 2018, in Indianapolis.

(Right) Gov Holcomb and First Lady Janet Holcomb join MC Hammer, Warden Lashelle Turner, Beverly Parenti, Department of Corrections Commissioner Chris Redlitz, Rob Carter, and students during a ribbon cutting for the Last Mile program on April 5, 2018, at the Indiana Women's Prison in Indianapolis. The program teaches incarcerated individuals tech and social skills.

Gov. Holcomb and Scott Swan on the Channel 13 set during the Mini Marathon on May 5, 2018, in Indianapolis.

Gov. Holcomb and First Lady Janet Holcomb with Israeli Prime Minister Benjamin Netanyahu during an economic development trip on May 10, 2018, in Tel Aviv, Israel.

Gov. Holcomb, Speaker Brian Bosma, and Senate Leader David Long catch up on some homework while traveling during an economic development trip on May 21, 2018, in Europe.

(Far left) Gov. Holcomb inserts a written prayer in the Western Wall during an economic development trip on May 9, 2018, in Jerusalem, Israel.

(Left) Gov. Holcomb hands out ceremonial signing pens with Rep. Doug Gutwein after signing HEA 1017 into law on May 11, 2018, in Carmel. The measure requires spinal muscular atrophy and severe combined immunodeficiency to be added to the list of screenings newborns receive in Indiana.

(Above) Gov. Holcomb shakes hands with Slovak Minister of Economy Peter Žiga after signing an MOU to build defense and academic relationships, as well as investment, trade, and workforce development on May 21, 2018, in Bratislava, Slovakia.

(Right) Gov. Holcomb cuts a ribbon to celebrate the inaugural Flight #500 from Paris to Indianapolis on May 25, 2018, in Paris, France.

(Left) Gov. Holcomb with lifelong friend, then President of Penske Racing Tim Cindric, on the track at the Indianapolis Motor Speedway before the Indy 500 on May 27, 2018, in Indianapolis.

(Below) Gov. Holcomb celebrates with executives from Nippon Steel at the grand opening of a new 150,000-square-foot facility on July 18, 2018, in Shelbyville.

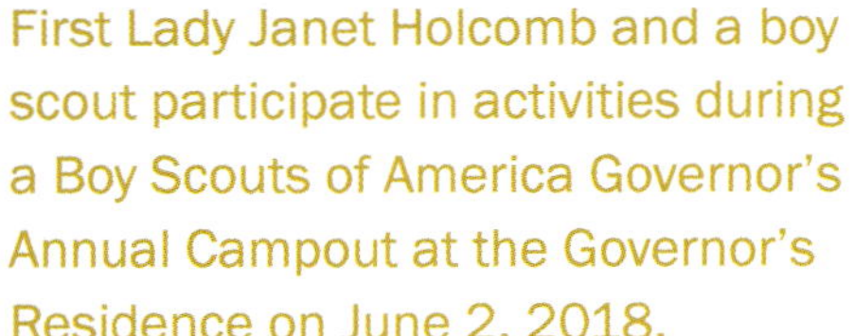

First Lady Janet Holcomb and a boy scout participate in activities during a Boy Scouts of America Governor's Annual Campout at the Governor's Residence on June 2, 2018.

Gov. Holcomb downs a glass of milk to celebrate the grand opening of Walmart's massive new milk processing plant on June 13, 2018, in Fort Wayne.

Gov. Holcomb walks on a trail with Kendallville Mayor SuzAnne Handshoe on June 13, 2018, in Kendallville.

Gov. Holcomb on the front porch of Grouseland outside the home of William Henry Harrison during an event on June 16, 2018, in Vincennes.

Gov. Holcomb cheers for a made basket on the Governor's Court during the court unveiling with the DeKalb County Special Olympics team on Aug. 18, 2018, at the Governor's Residence.

Gov. Holcomb enjoys a delicious shake at the counter of Emery's Ice Cream Shop on Aug. 9, 2018, in Corydon.

Gov. Holcomb sees a demonstration at Commodore Manufacturing on Aug. 10, 2018, in Leopold.

(Left) Gov. Holcomb delivers remarks after being recognized as the International Citizen of the Year by the International Center on Aug. 23, 2018, in Indianapolis.

(Below) Gov. Holcomb congratulates members of the Warren Central High School Girls Basketball team on their first state title on July 20, 2018, in the Governor's Office.

Gov. Holcomb addresses USS *Indiana* crew members before the ship's commissioning ceremony on Sept. 28, 2018, in Port Canaveral, FL.

Gov. Holcomb makes a quick stop at Schimpff's Confectionery on Sept. 7, 2018, in Jeffersonville.

Gov. Holcomb, Secretary of Commerce Jim Schellinger, and race car driver Sara Fisher point out the Indiana logo on a Dallara race car during an economic development trip on Sept. 21, 2018, in Italy.

Gov. Holcomb catches up with West Lafayette Mayor John Dennis and Lafayette Mayor Tony Roswarski before a Next Level Connections announcement on Sept. 6, 2018, in West Lafayette.

Sweetwater Founder and Chairman Chuck Surack and Gov. Holcomb, as well as the late Fort Wayne Mayor Tom Henry, break ground on an expansion of Sweetwater's footprint on Oct. 2, 2018, in Fort Wayne.

Gov. Holcomb and an Indiana delegation meet with OMR automotive executives during an economic development trip on Sept. 20, 2018, in Brescia, Italy.

Gov. Holcomb and Department of Natural Resources Director Cameron Clark applaud longtime DNR surveyor Bob Vollmer, who worked for DNR for fifty-five years and retired at 102 years of age. He was recognized at the Governor's long-term employee event on Dec. 3, 2018, in the Statehouse.

Gov. Holcomb and First Dog Henry at Dull's Tree Farm on Nov. 21, 2018, near Thorntown.

Gov. Holcomb with members of the Indiana Legislative Black Caucus on Jan. 17, 2019, in the Governor's Office.

First Dog Henry Holcomb and Blue from the Colts on Jan. 2, 2019, in the Governor's Office.

Gov. Holcomb gives a tour of his presidential signature collection to WIBC reporter Eric Berman on Feb. 11, 2019, at the Governor's Residence.

Gov. Holcomb has fun with mascots from Indiana professional basketball teams promoting "Basketball Day" in Indiana on Jan. 18, 2019, in Indianapolis.

Gov. Holcomb gets tips from Brandt Baughman, region manager of Indiana State Parks, and Potawatomi Inn General Manager Emily Burris on Feb. 8, 2019, before racing down the toboggan run at Pokagon State Park.

Gov. Holcomb and Ray Shearer of the USS *Indiana* Commissioning Committee show crew members from the USS *Indianapolis* the wood atop the governor's desk, which came from the decking on the former USS *Indiana*, on Jan. 15, 2019.

Gov. Holcomb and FSSA Secretary Dr. Jennifer Walthall with members of Self Advocates of Monroe County on Feb. 14, 2019, in the Governor's Office.

Gov. Holcomb crowns Ms. Wheelchair Indiana Shauna Wilson with a tiara, posing with her family on March 21, 2019, at the Governor's Residence.

Gov. Holcomb and Huntingburg Mayor Denny Spinner visit the famous Stellar Park, where the baseball movie *A League of Their Own* was filmed, on March 23, 2019, in Huntingburg.

(Above) Gov. Holcomb announces a Career Pathway Program and Next Level Training partnership between AAR Corp. and Vincennes University on Jan. 31, 2019, at the Vincennes University Aviation Center in Indianapolis.

(Above) Gov. Holcomb sings along to "God Bless America" led by Everett Greene during the Indiana Leadership Prayer Breakfast on March 26, 2019, in Indianapolis.

(Right) Gov. Holcomb sits next to University of Southern Indiana's 4th President Ronald Rochon during his inauguration ceremony on April 5, 2019, in Evansville.

(Far right) Gov. Holcomb raises the Indy 500 flag on April 12, 2019, at the Governor's Residence.

Gov. Holcomb speaks during a jobs announcement for SAAB on May 8, 2019, at Purdue University in West Lafayette.

Gov. Holcomb stopped by the State Budget Agency office on the last day of the legislative session, April 24, 2019, at the Statehouse.

Gov. Holcomb plays tag with cancer survivor C. J. Moreno during a Make-A-Wish visit on May 13, 2019, in the Governor's Office.

Former football coach and Zotec team member Lou Holtz, Gov. Holcomb, and Zotec CEO Scott Law share a laugh during a groundbreaking ceremony for a facility expansion and announcement of 300 new job openings on April 9, 2019, at their headquarters in Carmel.

Gov. Holcomb signs HEA 1284, which strengthened Indiana's "stand your ground" laws, while on stage at the National Rifle Association's Leadership Forum on April 26, 2019, in Indianapolis.

Gov. Holcomb hoopin' it up on April 30, 2019, at Seymour High School in Seymour.

Gov. Holcomb speaks at a memorial service for former US Sen. Birch Bayh on May 1, 2019, in the Statehouse.

(Above) Gov. Holcomb walks into the Statehouse behind the casket of former US Sen. Richard Lugar during his memorial service on May 14, 2019.

(Left) Gov. Holcomb with IHSAA State Champion basketball teams from Carmel, Silver Creek, Fort Wayne Blackhawk Christian, Hamilton Southeastern, Northwestern, Oak Hill, and Marquette Catholic High Schools on May 17, 2019, on the basketball court at the Governor's Residence.

Gov. Holcomb delivers a ceremonial first pitch strike as Hall of Famer Ryne Sandberg looks on before the Midwest League All Star Game on June 18, 2019, at Four Winds Field in South Bend.

Gov. Holcomb helps unveil the new sign for the Indiana Dunes National Park alongside US Sen. Todd Young on May 28, 2019, in Gary.

Owner, President, and CEO of WISH-TV DuJuan McCoy and Gov. Holcomb catch up at the Indiana Black Expo Corporate Luncheon on July 19, 2019, in Indianapolis.

Gov. Holcomb eats lunch with Indiana National Guard members during the Boy Scouts of America Governor's Annual Campout on June 8, 2019, on the grounds of the Governor's Residence. First Dog Henry waits for scraps.

Gov. Holcomb drives a truck on the test track before a groundbreaking for a new Innovation Center at Allison Transmission on June 14, 2019, in Indianapolis.

DCS Director Terry Stigdon introduces Gov. Holcomb before signing HB 1006, which extended collaborative care services eligibility for older youth in foster care and established limits on family case manager caseloads, on June 13, 2019, in the Statehouse.

(Top left) Gov. Holcomb gets a laugh before signing HEA 1394, which established the Indiana Women's Suffrage Centennial Commission, on June 13, 2019, in the Governor's Office.

(Top right) Gov. Holcomb, First Lady Janet Holcomb, and First Dog Henry celebrate the opening of a new Blue Buffalo manufacturing plant on June 17, 2019, in Richmond.

(Left) President Donald J. Trump welcomes the 103rd Indianapolis 500 Champion Simon Pagenaud, Team Penske owner Roger Penske and team members, as well as Gov. Holcomb, Vice President Mike Pence, IndyCar CEO Mark Miles, and the Borg-Warner trophy on June 10, 2019, to the Oval Office.

Gov. Holcomb and Consul General of Japan in Chicago Naoki Ito plant an Okame Cherry Tree in honor of Consul General Ito at the Governor's Residence on Aug. 21, 2019.

Gov. Holcomb addresses a crowd at Mount Vernon High School before signing HB 1004, which mandated disaster and active shooter drills, on Aug. 9, 2019, in Mount Vernon.

Gov. Holcomb visits the BMV booth at the State Fair and gets to saddle up on a "Ride Safe Indiana" trike on Aug. 5, 2019, at the State Fairgrounds in Indianapolis.

Gov. Holcomb signs a kid's forehead during the first day of the Indiana State Fair on Aug. 2, 2019, in Indianapolis.

Gov. Holcomb takes a tour of Spring Mill State Park with DNR Director Dan Bortner on Aug. 23, 2019.

Gov. Holcomb presents George Rapp with the Sachem Award on Aug. 27, 2019, at the Indiana State Museum in Indianapolis.

Gov. Holcomb in a bilateral meeting with Republic of Korea Prime Minister Lee Nak-yon on Sept. 4, 2019, during an economic development trip to South Korea.

Gov. Holcomb welcomes the Forbes AgTech Summit to Indiana on Sept. 19, 2019, in Indianapolis.

Gov. Holcomb writes the name of his best teacher on Aug. 27, 2019, in Indianapolis.

Gov. Holcomb and Rep. Todd Huston talk to students at Fishers High School after an announcement by Gov. Holcomb on a new approach and investment in tobacco cessation efforts aimed at youth vaping on Aug. 29, 2019, in Fishers.

WNBA Commissioner Cathy Engelbert talks to First Lady Janet Holcomb, Gov. Holcomb, and Notre Dame Women's Basketball Coach Muffet McGraw during a reception for the Indiana Fever on Aug. 27, 2019, at the Governor's Residence.

Gov. Holcomb places the first legal sports bet on Sept. 1, 2019, at the Indiana Grand Casino in Shelbyville. He wagered on the Colts and Pacers to win their championships and for the Fever to win the game that night.

Gov. Holcomb talks to law enforcement members before the Indiana Fraternal Order of Police Law Enforcement Memorial Service on Sept. 19, 2019, outside the Statehouse.

Gov. Holcomb holds a sloth on Sept. 20, 2019, during a staff trip to the Indianapolis Zoo.

Gov. Holcomb, Sherry Lyles, and Indiana's new Adjutant General Dale Lyles during a pinning ceremony on Oct. 15, 2019, in the Governor's Office.

Gov. Holcomb plays Skee-Ball at McWhiggins Wonder Emporium on Oct. 10, 2019, in Madison.

Gov. Holcomb and Indiana Department of Transportation Commissioner Joe McGuinness with elected representatives and town and county officials for a Community Crossings award event on Oct. 10, 2019, in Madison.

Advisor to the President Ivanka Trump joins US Secretary of Commerce Wilbur Ross, Apple CEO Tim Cook, Walmart CEO Doug McMillon, and Gov. Holcomb for an American Workforce Policy Advisory Board meeting on Dec. 5, 2019, at the Indiana Women's Prison in Indianapolis.

Gov. Holcomb takes a selfie onstage during the 92nd FFA National Convention on Oct. 30, 2019, in Indianapolis.

Gov. Holcomb and First Lady Janet Holcomb try the Eva Kor virtual reality experience thanks to the Indiana Rotary Foundation on Oct. 30, 2019, at the Governor's Residence.

Gov. Holcomb breaks ground with members of the White River State Park Development Commission for the Live Nation Amphitheatre venue on Oct. 16, 2019, in Indianapolis.

Gov. Holcomb with participants at a youth anti-tobacco action rally on Jan. 27, 2020, in the Statehouse.

Gov. Holcomb talks to Gerry Dick on the set of Inside Indiana Business on Jan. 30, 2020, in Indianapolis.

Gov. Holcomb reads *What Do You Do With An Idea?* to fourth graders from Loper Elementary School for Read Across America Day on March 2, 2020, in the Governor's Office.

Gov. Holcomb talks to Amish constituents on Jan. 22, 2020, in the Governor's Office.

First Lady Janet Holcomb, Gov. Holcomb, and First Dog Henry Holcomb meet Butler Blue IV on Jan. 24, 2020, at the Governor's Residence.

Executive Director for Drug Prevention, Treatment, and Enforcement Jim McClelland and Gov. Holcomb share a laugh for his farewell gathering on Jan. 6, 2020, in the Governor's Office. McClelland was the state's first such director.

Gov. Holcomb, on a cold winter morning inside the old General Electric building in Fort Wayne, announced that Do It Best Corp. would be the anchor tenant in the new Electric Works campus. The announcement was made on Feb. 13, 2020, in Fort Wayne.

Gov. Holcomb greets former President Barack Obama on Feb. 15, 2020, during the NBA Newsmaker Breakfast in Chicago as part of the NBA All-Star weekend.

Indiana Executive Director for Drug Prevention, Treatment, and Enforcement Doug Huntsinger, Indiana State Museum and Historic Sites President Cathy Ferree, Gov. Holcomb, and Indiana State Museum Board Member Bill Browne walk through the State Museum's new interactive exhibit about the opioid crisis and recovery on Jan. 31, 2020, in Indianapolis.

Gov. Holcomb speaks with McDonald's employees and Ivy Tech students on Jan. 9, 2020, in Indianapolis. Holcomb was there to announce the educational benefits provided to McDonald's employees by Owner Operators Jim and Pamela Poore, who also decided to further their education through discounted tuition and benefits at Ivy Tech.

(Above) Gov. Holcomb meets with his cabinet at the beginning of the COVID-19 pandemic on March 15, 2020, in the Governor's Office.

(Right) First Lady Janet Holcomb speaks during a ceremony for Accenture International Women's Day on March 6, 2020, in the Statehouse.

(Far right) Gov. Holcomb speaks at the Indiana Farmers Coliseum to announce the 2020 State Fair theme of "Celebrating the State that Grew the Game of Basketball" on March 10, 2020.

A group gathered at the Governor's Residence on April 18, 2020, to protest Gov. Holcomb's COVID-19 stay-at-home order.

First Dog Henry and First Lady Janet Holcomb on April 7, 2020, in the Governor's Office.

Gov. Holcomb participates in a discussion about preparations and response to COVID-19 on March 11, 2020.

Gov. Holcomb outlines state actions in response to the COVID-19 pandemic. On March 16, 2020, he issued an executive order to institute measures protecting Hoosiers from the virus.

Gov. Holcomb on stage with Fiat Chrysler COO Mark Stewart in Kokomo, where Fiat Chrysler announced the plant's name change from Indiana Transmission Plant II to the Kokomo Engine Plant on March 5, 2020.

Gov. Holcomb and First Dog Henry on May 20, 2020, at the Governor's Residence.

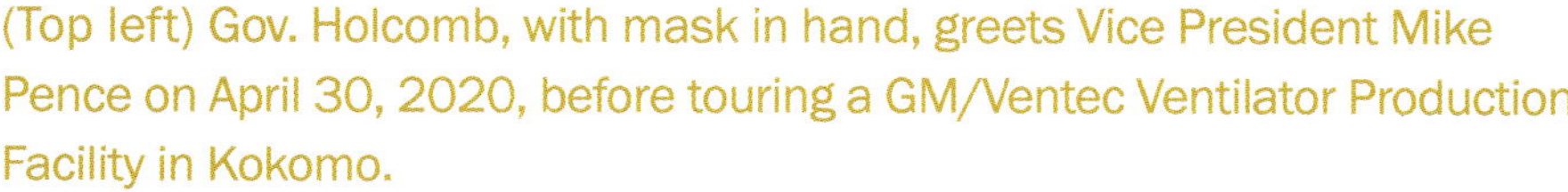

(Top left) Gov. Holcomb, with mask in hand, greets Vice President Mike Pence on April 30, 2020, before touring a GM/Ventec Ventilator Production Facility in Kokomo.

(Top right) The beginning of First Lady Janet Holcomb's chicken coop project on May 1, 2020, at the Governor's Residence.

(Right) Gov. Holcomb speaks to members of the press after an American Workforce Policy Advisory Board Meeting on June 26, 2020, outside the White House.

Gov. Holcomb and USS *Indianapolis* survivor Edgar Harrell on July 24, 2020, during a ceremony to transfer a Congressional Gold Medal from the United States Mint to Survivors, Lost at Sea family, and the Indiana War Memorial in Indianapolis.

Gov. Holcomb with DNR Director Dan Bortner and State Forester John Seifert after announcing two new state forests—Ravinia State Forest and Mountain; and Tea State Forest—on Aug. 14, 2020, in Morgan County.

Gov. Holcomb snapped this shot of Henry on his lap watching the Indy 500 on Aug. 23, 2020, on the back porch at the Governor's Residence.

Gov. Holcomb signs a document for newly appointed Indiana Court of Appeals Judge Leanna Weissmann on Sept. 1, 2020, in the Governor's Office.

Gov. Holcomb with citizens of Scott County who traveled to the Governor's Office to celebrate their county's bicentennial on Oct. 5, 2020.

Gov. Holcomb and members of the Clarksville Town Council do their best Abbey Road impression before cutting the ribbon for the Discovery Trail on Sept. 3, 2020, in Clarksville.

Gov. Holcomb and the Clarksville Town Council help cut the ribbon for the grand opening celebrating the Discovery Trail, a new path that connects the Ohio River Greenway and several nearby schools, neighborhoods, and commercial corridors throughout Clarksville and southern Indiana on Sept. 3, 2020.

Gov. Holcomb plays with Amy and Brent Fox's adopted child on Sept. 20, 2020, in the Governor's Office during an adoption event.

Gov. Holcomb with the 2020 Sachem Award winner Reggie Jones, who was recognized for his role as a business and community leader on Sept. 8, 2020, at the Indiana State Museum.

An image captured at a Langham Logistics site in Indianapolis where the state stored personal protective equipment, including face masks made in Indiana by Indiana Face Mask in Rensselaer on Oct. 27, 2020.

Gov. Holcomb gets ready to turn dirt in Munster at an event to recognize funding to build the West Lake Corridor Project on Oct. 28, 2020.

Gov. Holcomb snapped a photo of his niece shooting baskets at the barn at Aynes House on Dec. 26, 2020, in Brown County State Park.

Gov. Holcomb cuts the ribbon at the opening ceremony for the Don Strauss Animal Science Education Center on the campus of Huntington University on Nov. 16, 2020, in Huntington.

Gov. Holcomb poses with members of his family after his second inaugural ceremony on Jan. 11, 2021, in Indianapolis.

(Right) Gov. Holcomb signs inauguration programs before his second inaugural ceremony on Jan. 11, 2021, in Indianapolis.

(Below) Gov. Holcomb delivers his 2021 State of the State Address virtually on Jan. 19, 2021, from the WFYI Studios in Indianapolis.

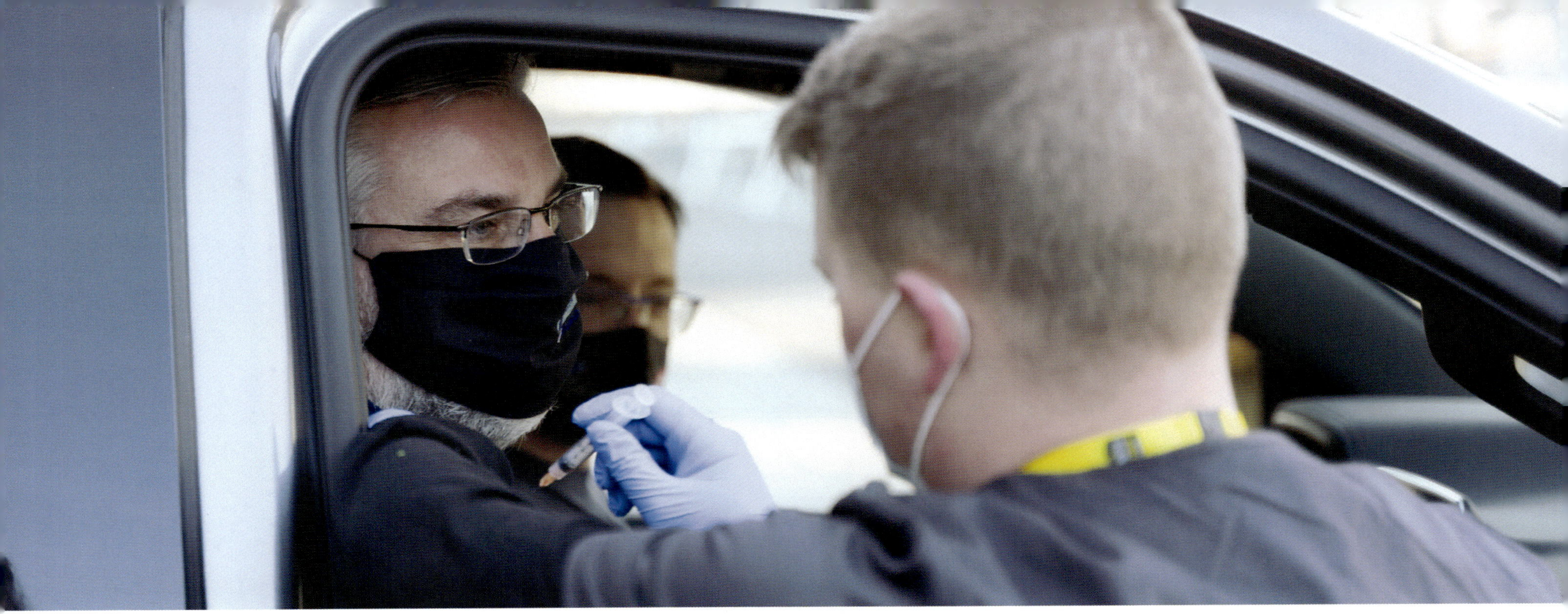

(Above) Gov. Holcomb receives his COVID-19 vaccination along with IMS President Doug Boles on March 5, 2021, during a drive-through vaccination event at the Indianapolis Motor Speedway.

(Right) Gov. Holcomb delivers remarks before a ribbon-cutting ceremony for the new global headquarters of iA on March 9, 2021, in Indianapolis.

(Far right) Gov. Holcomb shoots baskets in the snow on Feb. 22, 2021, at the Governor's Residence.

Gov. Holcomb delivers a statewide address from his desk on March 23, 2021.

Gov. Holcomb signs a bill with a pen made from the famous Eisenhower Tree at Augusta National Golf Club on April 1, 2021, in the Governor's Office.

Gov. Holcomb enjoys some Indiana popcorn as part of signing a law making popcorn the state's official snack on April 15, 2021, in the Governor's Office.

(Right) Gov. Holcomb hands out ceremonial signing pens after signing Senate Enrolled Act 1, which provides civil tort immunity for damages arising from COVID-19 on the premises owned or operated by a person. The Act defines "COVID-19 protective product" and provides civil tort immunity for harm that results from the design, manufacture, labeling, sale, distribution, or donation of a COVID-19 protective product, except for an act or omission that constitutes gross negligence or willful or wanton misconduct. The event was held on Feb. 18, 2021, in the Governor's Office.

(Far right) Legislative Director Chris Creighton waits by the window while Gov. Holcomb signs bills on April 29, 2021, in the Governor's Office.

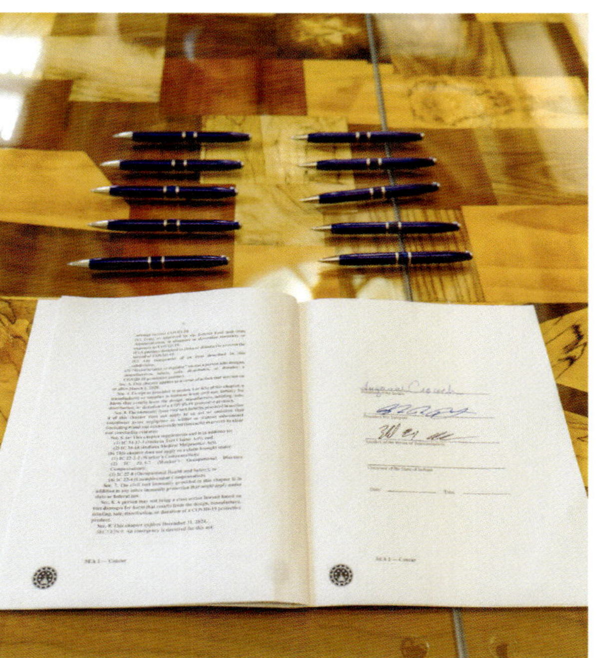

(Far left) Gov. Holcomb, Milwaukee Tool President of Power Tools Shane Moll, and Greenwood Mayor Mark Myers cut the ribbon on Milwaukee Tool's new tool service hub in Greenwood on May 6, 2021.

(Left) Gov. Holcomb gifts a tie to Pokagon Band of Potawatomi Indians of Michigan and Indiana Tribal Council Chairman Matthew Wesaw after a ceremonial signing of a bill that codified the compact between the Pokagon Band of Potawatomi Indians and the state, providing for the conduct of tribal gaming, on May 4, 2021, in South Bend.

Gov. Holcomb meets with Indiana's first Chief Equity, Inclusion, and Opportunity Officer Karrah Herring on April 15, 2021, in the Governor's Office.

Gov. Holcomb moves some dirt with Bobby Rahal, Mike Lannigan, and Zionsville Mayor Emily Styron to celebrate the groundbreaking of Rahal Letterman Lanigan Racing's state-of-the-art racing headquarters on May 18, 2021, in Zionsville.

Governor Holcomb traveled to Israel at the invitation of Prime Minister Benjamin Netanyahu in May of 2021 after a ceasefire ended a period of intense fighting between Israel and Hamas in Gaza. While there, he and Indiana Republican Party Chairman Kyle Hupfer visited an Iron Dome battery and toured areas recently affected by rocket attacks.

Gov. Holcomb at a groundbreaking ceremony to celebrate the expansion of greenhouse space at INARI on June 2, 2021, in West Lafayette.

Gov. Holcomb tours a vehicle seat manufacturing facility run by Japanese-owned NHK after a groundbreaking ceremony for an expansion of their Indiana footprint on June 16, 2021, in Frankfort.

Gov. Holcomb and IMS Owner Roger Penske during Carb Day on May 28, 2021, at the Indianapolis Motor Speedway.

(Far left) Gov. Holcomb watches a young man wearing a Larry Bird jersey shoot baskets during the opening day of the Hoosier Court on June 23, 2021, in Knightstown.

(Left) Gov. Holcomb delivers remarks with US Sen. Todd Young during a press conference in Fishers on June 18, 2021, to celebrate the passing of the Endless Frontiers Act, which invests in emerging technology.

Gov. Holcomb awards the 2021 Sachem to Jim Morris on June 25, 2021, during the Sachem Ceremony in Indianapolis.

Gov. Holcomb meets members of the US Air Force stationed in Qatar on July 8, 2021, during an economic development trip.

Gov. Holcomb and Press Secretary Erin Murphy-Verplank belly up to the Indiana Maple Syrup bar on July 30, 2021, during the opening day at the Indiana State Fair in Indianapolis.

Gov. Holcomb and Westfield Mayor Andy Cook turn dirt at the groundbreaking for West Fork Whiskey, a local craft whiskey distillery on July 27, 2021, in Westfield.

Gov. Holcomb and Little League International CEO Stephen Keener acknowledge the singing of the National Anthem by a little leaguer from Zionsville on June 26, 2021, during the Little League Central Region headquarters opening ceremony in Whitestown.

Gov. Holcomb cuts the ribbon at the revamped Ivy Tech Kokomo campus on Aug. 4, 2021.

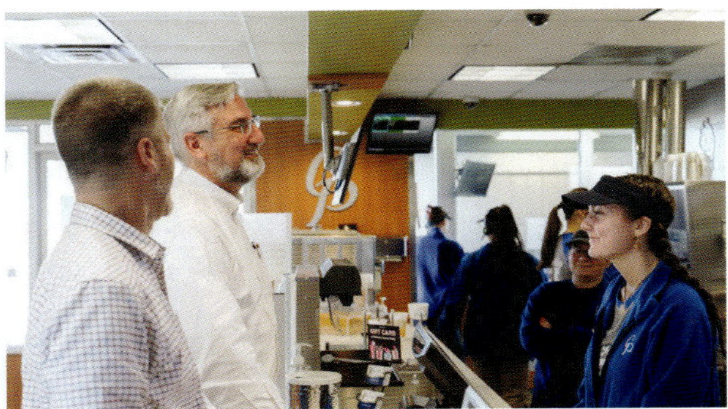

(Above) Gov. Holcomb stops at his favorite Kokomo ice cream place—Cone Palace—with Howard County Commissioner Paul Wyman on Aug. 4, 2021.

(Left) Gov. Holcomb helps unveil the Jeffrey A. Stout Memorial Highway sign on Aug. 4, 2021, in Russiaville.

65th BIENNIAL CONFERENCE
ATIONAL FRATERNAL ORDER OF POLIC

Gov. Holcomb cuts the ribbon to start gaming on Aug. 5, 2021, at the Pokagon Band's Four Winds Casino in South Bend.

(Above) Gov. Holcomb spends a day at the State Fair on Aug. 7, 2021, in Indianapolis.

(Facing page) Gov. Holcomb delivers welcome remarks during the National Fraternal Order of Police Conference on Aug. 16, 2021, in Indianapolis.

Gov. Holcomb surprises Rep. Steve Davisson with a Sagamore of the Wabash award in front of family and supporters on Aug. 11, 2021, in the Statehouse. Davisson would pass away just over a month later.

"Today is more proof that Indiana will continue to play a key role in the global energy sector, with clean, renewable energy sources for generations of Hoosiers to come. Today, I joined Israeli officials, Doral Renewables executives, and local leaders in Starke County for an electrifying day as we broke ground on Mammoth Solar—the largest US solar farm."

–Governor Eric J. Holcomb

Governor Holcomb breaks ground with Doral officials at a ceremony on Oct. 14, 2021, to mark the start of construction of their Mammoth Solar project located in Starke County, Indiana, set to be the country's largest solar farm. Holcomb heralded Doral Renewables' "significant" investment in the state for creating jobs for local residents and providing renewable power for the Midwest region. *Image courtesy of Doral Renewables/Eric Holcomb.*

Gov. Holcomb met Afghan refugees during his visit, on Sept. 8, 2021, to Camp Atterbury.

Gov. Holcomb and Adjutant General Dale Lyles aboard a Blackhawk on Sept. 8, 2021, on their way to Camp Atterbury.

Gov. Holcomb snaps in a selfie on Aug. 18, 2021, after celebrating Indiana Traffic Safety All-Stars at Victory Field in Indianapolis.

Gov. Holcomb shakes hands with a Rolls-Royce employee during a tour of the manufacturing campus on Aug. 11, 2021, in Indianapolis. The company invested $400 million to revitalize the facility.

Gov. Holcomb, First Dog Henry, and Chief of Staff Earl Goode talk business in September 2021 in the backyard at the Governor's Residence.

Gov. Holcomb and US Sen. Todd Young approve of the 2022 Honda Civic Hatchback on Sept. 20, 2021, in Greensburg at the line-off event for the car.

Gov. Holcomb on a tour of the new production facility at Umbarger Feed Mill on Sept. 24, 2021, in Franklin.

Gov. Holcomb signs his name to an electric transmission after signing a bill that established the Electric Vehicle Product Commission on Oct. 7, 2021, at the Stellantis Transmission Plant II in Kokomo.

Gov. Holcomb and Ferdinand News Editor Kathy Tretter enjoy meeting on Nov. 9, 2021, during the Jasper Chamber of Commerce annual luncheon. Tretter and the governor became well-acquainted during the COVID-19 public health crisis because she participated in almost every virtual COVID-19 update the governor provided to Hoosiers.

(Far left) Gov. Holcomb and First Lady Janet Holcomb pose with a trick-or-treater on Oct. 31, 2021. The Holcombs were dressed as Indiana icons for Halloween at the Governor's Residence.

(Left) State Trooper Lieutenant and Governor's Detail lead Scott Pratt, dressed as Santa, with First Lady Janet Holcomb before the Hoosier Holidays celebration in the Statehouse on Dec. 6, 2021.

(Right) Gov. Holcomb makes the rounds during the Performance Racing Industry's annual convention on Dec. 10, 2021, inside the Indianapolis Convention Center.

(Far right) Gov. Holcomb talks to Indiana Department of Administration employees on Dec. 7, 2021, at the IDOA Christmas party in Indianapolis.

Gov. Holcomb with scouts from across Indiana on Dec. 16, 2021, in Lucas Oil Stadium for the Governor's Luncheon for Scouting.

Gov. Holcomb with Rep. Randy Frye and members of the Indiana Volunteer Firefighters Association on Feb. 21, 2022, in the Governor's Office.

Gov. Holcomb meets with Department of Correction staff and participants in the Hoosier Initiative for Re-Entry program to celebrate the tenth anniversary of the program on Feb. 17, 2022, in the Governor's Office.

Gov. Holcomb thanks Sgt. Maj. Robert Brown for his service on Jan. 13, 2022. Brown is a veteran of three wars—World War II, Korea, and Vietnam—and received a Sagamore of the Wabash award in the Governor's Office.

Gov. Holcomb catching up with the (now late) Congresswoman Jackie Walorski on Jan. 26, 2022, in the Governor's Office.

Gov. Holcomb inspects Justin Schoenefeld's Olympic Gold Medal from the 2022 Winter Games on Feb. 28, 2022, in the Governor's Office.

Gov. Holcomb and Chief of Staff Earl Goode catch up with US Ambassador to the Vatican Joe Donnelly on March 1, 2022, in the Governor's Office.

First Dog Henry gives some straight talk to Gov. Holcomb over coffee on March 2, 2022, in the Governor's Office.

First Lady Janet Holcomb and First Dog Henry on March 2, 2022, during a meet and greet with elementary and middle school students from Danville in the Governor's Office.

Gov. Holcomb and Indiana Department of Workforce Development Commissioner Fred Payne review data on March 8, 2022, during a meeting in the Governor's Office.

The Hanover College Panther takes over the governor's desk during a meeting between Gov. Holcomb and Hanover College President Lake Lambert on March 2, 2022, in the Governor's Office.

Four-time Indy 500 Champion Hélio Castroneves and Gov. Holcomb with the Borg-Warner trophy commemorating Castroneves's latest win on March 3, 2022, during an unveiling ceremony in the Statehouse.

State Fire Marshal Joel Thacker and Gov. Holcomb talk to the press on March 16, 2022, after an event in Greensburg to kick off an effort to collect and dispose of certain firefighting materials.

(Right) Gov. Holcomb and Ukrainian Ambassador to the US Oksana Markarova on March 10, 2022, in Washington, DC, discussing the Russian invasion of Ukraine.

(Far right) Gov. Holcomb and *Indy Star* reporter Greg Doyel shoot hoops on March 14, 2022, during an interview about the governor's passion for basketball at the Governor's Residence court.

(Above) Gov. Holcomb with the Zionsville Chamber of Commerce during their annual lunch on April 18, 2022, at Traders Point Creamery.

(Far left) Gov. Holcomb and First Lady Janet Holcomb place a wreath near the Gate of Freedom on March 28, 2022, during an economic development trip to Slovakia.

(Left) Gov. Holcomb surprises ninety-five-year-old Helena Rikke on April 4, 2022, with a Sagamore of the Wabash award. Rikke worked for the state from 1979 until her retirement in 2022.

Gov. Holcomb, SAAB CEO Micael Johansson, and Secretary of Commerce Brad Chambers on April 25, 2022, during an economic development trip to Sweden.

Gov. Holcomb visits the construction site of the new Fall Creek Pavilion on May 13, 2022, at the Indiana State Fairgrounds.

Gov. Holcomb gifts an Indiana-themed racing helmet to Israeli Minister of Foreign Affairs Yair Lapid on March 31, 2022, during an economic development trip to Israel.

Gov. Holcomb with leaders of the Indiana Asian American Alliance on May 6, 2022, during a visit to promote Asian American Pacific Islander Heritage Month in the Governor's Office.

Gov. Holcomb with United Kingdom member of parliament Penny Mordaunt and Secretary of Commerce Brad Chambers on April 27, 2022, during an economic development trip to the United Kingdom.

Secretary of Commerce Brad Chambers, Gov. Holcomb, and Elanco CEO Jeff Simmons look toward a former General Motors Stamping Plant site west of downtown Indianapolis on April 12, 2022. Elanco is building its new headquarters at the site.

Gov. Holcomb addresses the auction crowd on May 13, 2022, during the Mecum Auction at the Indiana State Fairgrounds.

Gov. Holcomb moderates a panel that included Penske Corporation Chairman and CEO Roger Penske, Bridgestone Americas President and CEO Paolo Ferrari, NTT Data Services Group President Chris Merdon, and Shell Executive Vice President Carlos Maurer on May 26, 2022, at the Global Economic Summit in Indianapolis.

Gov. Holcomb delivers remarks on May 25, 2022, at the Governor's Residence to announce Eli Lilly's plan to invest $2.1 billion to build two new manufacturing sites within Indiana's LEAP Lebanon Innovation and Research District.

Team Penske President Tim Cindric and Gov. Holcomb high-five on May 29, 2022, in the pits at the Indianapolis Motor Speedway before the Indy 500.

(Above) Gov. Holcomb drives a stake to commemorate the groundbreaking of the South Shore Double Track rail project on June 20, 2022, in Michigan City.

(Left) Gov. Holcomb cheers on Special Olympics Athletes and runners from law enforcement agencies around Indiana on June 10, 2022, as they run the Special Olympics Torch through downtown Indianapolis.

(Top left) Gov. Holcomb receives a tutorial before driving a tank on June 24, 2022, on the Vertex Company campus in Indianapolis.

(Top right) Gov. Holcomb watches a demonstration by the Guion Creek Middle School JagTech Robotics team on June 23, 2022, at the Governor's Residence.

(Right) Gov. Holcomb talks to Indiana's 106th Supreme Court Justice Steve David after awarding him a Sagamore of the Wabash award on Aug. 16, 2022. David announced his retirement that day in the Governor's Office.

Gov. Holcomb and Lilly Endowment Chairman and CEO Clay Robbins applaud on Aug. 18, 2022, during an event in Anderson to announce an investment of more than $100 million to support research-based reading instruction for Indiana students.

Taiwan President Tsai Ing-wen and Gov. Holcomb on Aug. 22, 2022, during an economic development trip to Taiwan.

Gov. Holcomb delivers remarks at a welcome banquet organized by the Taiwan Ministry of Foreign Affairs on Aug. 22, 2022, during an economic development trip to Taiwan.

Gov. Holcomb conducts a question and answer session in Indianapolis on Aug. 31, 2022, during a summit about the Indiana Next Level Fund, which makes targeted investments in venture capital funds and Indiana businesses.

Gov. Holcomb, Secretary of State Antony Blinken, Secretary of Commerce Gina Raimondo, US Senator Todd Young, and Purdue University President Mitch Daniels tour the Birck Center for Nanotechnology on the Purdue University campus on Sept. 13, 2022, during an event to celebrate the passage of the CHIPS and Science Act.

Gov. Holcomb and an Indiana delegation tour a Samsung SDI electric vehicle battery manufacturing facility on Aug. 25, 2022, during an economic development trip to South Korea.

Gov. Holcomb celebrates with the Japanese Governor of Gunma Prefecture Ichita Yamamoto on Sept. 8, 2022, after signing a memorandum of partnership and mutual cooperation in the Governor's Office.

First Dog Henry prepares for a groundbreaking event for Diamond Pet Foods in Rushville on Sept. 14, 2022.

Gov. Holcomb invites new Appeals Court Judge Peter Foley to the podium after announcing his appointment to the bench on Sept. 14, 2022, in the Governor's Office.

Gov. Holcomb admires the massive breaded pork tenderloin sandwich made for him on Sept. 16, 2022, during a competitive eating challenge at One Eyed Jack's in Winamac.

Gov. Holcomb receives a plate of biscuits and gravy on Sept. 24, 2022, during the Morgan County Bicentennial celebration in Waverly.

Gov. Holcomb, IEDC Chief of Staff David Rosenberg, and the Indiana delegation on Oct. 3, 2022, on a tour of Berlin during an economic development trip to Germany.

Gov. Holcomb announces a four-year extension of Horizon League Basketball Championships on Sept. 20, 2022, at the Indiana Farmers Coliseum in Indianapolis.

Gov. Holcomb with Bill and Gloria Gaither in Anderson on Sept. 23, 2022, dedicating a section of State Road 28 in their honor.

Gov. Holcomb tours construction progress during the rerouting of the North Split on Oct. 11, 2022, in Indianapolis.

Gov. Holcomb answered questions on Oct. 12, 2022, during a One Southern Indiana luncheon in New Albany.

Gov. Holcomb cracks a joke with attendees after delivering remarks on Oct. 29, 2022, during a VFW conference in Indianapolis.

Gov. Holcomb turns dirt on Oct. 19, 2022, to mark construction on a READI project in Princeton.

(Far left) First Lady Janet Holcomb and Gov. Holcomb dressed as the leg lamp and the pink nightmare from *A Christmas Story* for Halloween on Oct. 31, 2022, at the Governor's Residence.

(Left) Gov. Holcomb talks to Chief Justice Loretta Rush and new Indiana Supreme Court Justice Derek Molter on Nov. 1, 2022, in the Statehouse law library before Justice Molter's robing ceremony.

Gov. Holcomb on stage with Sullivan Mayor Clint Lamb on Nov. 2, 2022, during the Association of Indiana Municipalities Ideas Summit in French Lick.

Gov. Holcomb hears from construction workers at the Doral Mammoth Solar project on Nov. 3, 2022, during an event at the largest solar farm in the US, located in parts of Starke and Pulaski counties.

Gov. Holcomb celebrates the groundbreaking of WestGate One, a new facility to house semiconductor companies on Nov. 21, 2022, in Crane.

(Above) Gov. Holcomb, Fishers Mayor Scott Fadness, Michael Andretti, Dan Towruss, Mario Andretti, and Marissa Andretti celebrate the groundbreaking of Andretti Global's new headquarters on Dec. 6, 2022, in Indianapolis.

(Left) Gov. Holcomb talks to journalist Abdul-Hakim Shabazz on Dec. 16, 2022, in the Governor's Office.

(Top left) Gov. Holcomb on a camel during a trip to Egypt on Nov. 7, 2022.

(Above) Gov. Holcomb and 2022 Sachem Pat Koch of Holiday World and Splashin' Safari during her Sachem ceremony at Heritage Hills High School in Lincoln City on Dec. 9, 2022.

Gov. Holcomb signs the commission for newly appointed Indiana Court of Appeals Judge Dana Kenworthy on Dec. 21, 2022, in the Governor's Office.

Gov. Holcomb addresses kids, media, and mascots on Dec. 19, 2022, during an event to announce that the theme of the 2023 Indiana State Fair would be "The State that Grew the Game."

Gov. Holcomb and members of his cabinet on Jan. 23, 2023, in the Governor's Office.

Gov. Holcomb with IDOH Commissioner Kristina Box and former Sen. Luke Kenley on Jan. 26, 2023, before delivering remarks at a rally for Public Health Day in the Statehouse.

Gov. Holcomb announces his 2023 Next Level Agenda during a press conference at a Warren Township elementary school on Jan. 4, 2023.

Gov. Holcomb talks to Civil Air Patrol Cadets on Feb. 13, 2023, in the Governor's Office.

Gov. Holcomb talks to the sibling of a cancer survivor on Feb. 15, 2023, after delivering remarks in the Statehouse during Childhood Cancer Advocacy Day.

Gov. Holcomb, Department of Natural Resources Director Dan Bortner, and Fish and Wildlife Area Property Manager Kalli Dunn marvel at the flocks of snow geese at Goose Pond Fish and Wildlife Area on Feb. 2, 2023.

Gov. Holcomb with class of 2023 Jobs for America's Graduates students on March 17, 2023, at the JAG State Career Development Conference at Ivy Tech in Indianapolis.

Gov. Holcomb and Indiana University President Pam Whitten on Feb. 16, 2023, during a Greater Bloomington Chamber of Commerce luncheon.

Gov. Holcomb in prayer with pastors from across Indiana on March 7, 2023, in the Governor's Office.

Former First Lady Maggie Kernan smiles at a bust of her late husband Governor Joe Kernan on March 17, 2023, during an unveiling ceremony in the Statehouse.

Gov. Holcomb delivers remarks in the Union County Court House in Liberty on March 16, 2023, to announce that Full Throttle Fulfillment Solutions would locate in Union County.

Gov. Holcomb fills out his annual March Madness bracket on March 13, 2023, in the Governor's Office.

Gov. Holcomb laughs with Unbox CEO Erik Saelens and Consul General of Belgium Filip Vanden Bulcke on March 31, 2023, at the Governor's Residence.

Gov. Holcomb tours tornado damage with Sullivan Mayor Clint Lamb on April 1, 2023.

Gov. Holcomb meets IHSAA student interns on March 25, 2023, during the 3A and 4A Boys State Basketball Championships in Indianapolis.

(Far left) Gov. Holcomb on a call with Ukraine President Volodymyr Zelenskyy on April 4, 2023, during Zelenskyy's address to the National Governors Association.

(Left) Gov. Holcomb speaks to media at 3:21 a.m. on April 28, 2023, during a press conference at the conclusion of the 2023 legislative session in the Governor's Office.

Gov. Holcomb holds a Jim Morris Drive sign on April 18, 2023, during a lunch at the Governor's Residence to reveal the road near Riley Hospital would be renamed in Morris's honor.

Gov. Holcomb has fun with the Hagerstown Little League Baseball team, which represented the Great Lakes Region in the Little League World Series, on April 12, 2023, in the Governor's Office.

(Top) Gov. Holcomb signs bills with Chief of Staff Earl Goode, Legislative Director Tyler Ness, and Deputy Chief of Staff John Hammond on May 4, 2023, in the Governor's Office.

(Above) Gov. Holcomb cuts the ribbon on the River Greenway Trail with Department of Natural Resources Director Dan Bortner and Elkhart Mayor Rod Roberson on May 11, 2023, in Elkhart.

Kokomo High School basketball player Flory Bidunga rejects a shot on May 17, 2023, during a pickup game on the basketball court at the Governor's Residence.

Gov. Holcomb delivers remarks to celebrate the development underway on the Monon South Trail on May 5, 2023, in Salem.

Gov. Holcomb poses with leaders from South Bend and the South Bend Cubs after signing a bill that will help the city pay for improvements to its stadium and other sports or convention-related projects on May 4, 2023.

Gov. Holcomb signs two bills that address better mental health services during the Mental Health Roundtable Summit in Indianapolis on May 16, 2023.

Gov. Holcomb stands next to the new road signs welcoming drivers to Indiana with INDOT Commissioner Mike Smith, Indiana Destination Development Corporation CEO Elaine Bedel, and Indianapolis Motor Speedway President Doug Boles on May 18, 2023, after a press conference announcing new statewide signage at the Indianapolis Motor Speedway.

Gov. Holcomb with Trafalgar Police Officer Dustin Moody on May 17, 2023, during a meeting in the Governor's Office where Moody was awarded a Sagamore of the Wabash award for his distinguished service.

(Above left) Gov. Holcomb and Portuguese Secretary of State for International Trade and Foreign Investment Bernardo Ivo Cruz on June 5, 2023, during an economic development trip to Portugal.

(Above right) Gov. Holcomb walks a trail at the new Fern Station Nature Preserve in Putnam County with Central Indiana Land Trust President and CEO Cliff Chapman on June 16, 2023. The project included $3.1 million in state funding via the Next Level Conservation Trust.

(Far left) Gov. Holcomb delivers remarks on May 26, 2023, during the American Legion 500 Festival Memorial Service at the Indiana War Memorial in Indianapolis.

(Left) Gov. Holcomb and First Lady Janet Holcomb celebrate on May 28, 2023, as Josef Newgarden crosses the yard of bricks first to win the 107th running of the Indy 500.

(Below) Gov. Holcomb, along with Sen. Ed Charbonneau, Rep. Brad Barrett, and other stakeholders, signs legislation to provide more resources for public health services on May 24, 2023, in the Governor's Office.

(Top) Gov. Holcomb meets with the press on June 21, 2023, after the National Basketball Association announced the use of Lucas Oil Stadium for All-Star Saturday Night festivities during the 2024 All-Star Weekend in Indianapolis.

(Above) Gov. Holcomb, Indiana State Police Superintendent Doug Carter, and Indiana Department of Administration Commissioner Rebecca Holwerda celebrate the groundbreaking of a new Indiana State Police facility on June 23, 2023, near Evansville.

Gov. Holcomb is introduced on June 23, 2023, during an Evansville Chamber lunch at the University of Southern Indiana in Evansville.

Gov. Holcomb with the owners of Hard Truth Distillery on June 28, 2023, during a ribbon-cutting ceremony celebrating their new whiskey storage facility.

(Right) Gov. Holcomb shakes Judge Paul Felix's hand after the judge is appointed to the Court of Appeals on June 29, 2023, in the Governor's Office.

(Middle right) Gov. Holcomb welcomes innovators to Indiana for Rally, the largest cross-sector innovation conference in the world, on Aug. 29, 2023, in Indianapolis.

(Far right) Gov. Holcomb signs the commission for newly appointed Indiana Tax Court Judge Justin McAdam on July 11, 2023, in the Governor's Office.

(Bottom) Gov. Holcomb delivers remarks during the Midwest US–Japan Association conference on Sept. 10, 2023, during an economic development trip in Japan.

Gov. Holcomb, Indiana Department of Administration Commissioner Rebecca Holwerda, and Department of Correction Commissioner Christine Reagle celebrate the groundbreaking of the new Westville Correctional Facility on Sept. 28, 2023, in Westville.

Gov. Holcomb with New Hampshire Governor Chris Sununu and Salesforce cofounder and CEO Marc Benioff on Sept. 14, 2023, at Dreamforce in San Francisco.

Gov. Holcomb talks to a tourist near the Michigan City Lighthouse on Lake Michigan on Sept. 28, 2023.

(Above) Gov. Holcomb announces the launch of Treatment Atlas, Indiana's new addiction treatment locator on Sept. 29, 2023, in Indianapolis.

(Right) Gov. Holcomb tours the Electric Works Campus, home of the new headquarters for Do It Best Corp., on Oct. 5, 2023, in Fort Wayne.

(Top right) Gov. Holcomb delivers remarks with Michigan Governor Gretchen Whitmer and Wisconsin Governor Tony Evers on Oct. 13, 2023, during a gathering of the Great Lakes St. Lawrence Governors and Premiers in Cleveland, OH.

(Above) Gov. Holcomb and Adjutant General of the Indiana National Guard Dale Lyles turn dirt on Oct. 19, 2023, at a ceremony celebrating the groundbreaking of a new armory in Hamilton County.

Gov. Holcomb, Indiana Department of Administration Commissioner Rebecca Holwerda, and Department of Natural Resources Director Dan Bortner celebrate the start of construction on a new lodge at Potato Creek State Park on Oct. 19, 2023.

Gov. Holcomb, Indiana State Police Superintendent Doug Carter, and others celebrate the opening of the new Indiana State Police post and regional laboratory on Oct. 24, 2023, in Lowell.

Gov. Holcomb on stage with Jasper Chamber of Commerce Board President Ruger Kerstiens on Oct. 26, 2023, during a chamber lunch in Jasper.

Lauren Tomkiewicz, with Gov. Holcomb, family, and friends, reveals the redesigned Gold Star Family license plate on Oct. 30, 2023, in the Governor's Office.

(Right) Gov. Holcomb on stage with the 2023 Sachem, Albert Chen, who was recognized for his efforts in entrepreneurship, innovation, and leadership for the Asian American Alliance of Indiana and America China Society of Indiana on Nov. 2, 2023, in Carmel.

(Far right) Plant Manager Tim Hollender of Toyota Motor Manufacturing and Gov. Holcomb take a test drive of a new Lexus TX on Nov. 9, 2023, in Princeton.

Gov. Holcomb hugs new Indiana Comptroller Elise Nieshalla on Nov. 28, 2023, during her appointment announcement in Zionsville.

Gov. Holcomb with Stephanie Sanders on Nov. 23, 2023, during the Mozel Sanders Thanksgiving meal-packing event in Indianapolis.

Gov. Holcomb walks through Indiana Department of Transportation's new Kankakee Welcome Center on Oct. 24, 2023, off I-65.

Gov. Holcomb helps unload a pallet of pie plates at My Sugar Pie on Nov. 28, 2023, in Zionsville.

Gov. Holcomb meets with Indiana's public university presidents on Nov. 27, 2023, during a luncheon at the Governor's Residence.

The Adjutant General of Indiana Major Gen. Dale Lyles, Gov. Holcomb, and Indiana National Guardsman Phillip Craig on Nov. 15, 2023, at Camp Simba in Kenya.

Gov. Holcomb and Minister-President of Flanders Jan Jambon sign a memorandum of understanding on Dec. 8, 2023, in the Governor's Office.

Gov. Holcomb waves to students at West Central High School as his helicopter takes off from the school parking lot on Dec. 7, 2023.

Chief Justice Loretta Rush and Gov. Holcomb on Dec. 6, 2023, in the Indiana Supreme Court chamber.

(Top) Gov. Holcomb walks toward the La Crosse Public Library to announce recipients of the fourth round of Next Level Trails funding on Dec. 20, 2023, in La Crosse.

(Above) Gov. Holcomb invited essay contest winner Elin Edwards and her family to his office and gave her little brother a hat on Dec. 11, 2023, during Indiana's 207th Statehood Day in the Statehouse.

(Right) Gov. Holcomb delivers remarks to fourth graders invited to Indiana's 207th Statehood Day on Dec. 11, 2023, in the Statehouse.

Gov. Holcomb and other statewide elected officials sing “God Bless America” during the annual Public Servants Prayer Service on Jan. 8, 2024, in the Statehouse.

(Top) First Lady Janet Holcomb, portrait artist Russell Recchion, and Gov. Holcomb on Jan. 10, 2024, in the Governor's Office.

(Above) Gov. Holcomb inspects the track with Indiana State Fair staff after cutting the ribbon to open the indoor track and field facility on Jan. 19, 2024, inside Indiana Farm Bureau Fall Creek Pavilion at the State Fairgrounds.

Gov. Holcomb meets with the press after his 2024 Next Level Agenda announcement on Jan. 8, 2024, at the Indiana School for the Blind and Visually Impaired.

Secretary of Commerce David Rosenberg, Zimmer Biomet executive Jim Lancaster, and Gov. Holcomb tour a Zimmer Biomet facility on Jan. 18, 2024, in Warsaw.

(Above) Ontario Premier Doug Ford and Gov. Holcomb having a laugh before signing a memorandum of understanding on Jan. 23, 2024, while on an economic development trip to Canada.

(Right) Iowa Governor Kim Reynolds speaks to Gov. Holcomb after a press conference about the border crisis on Feb. 4, 2024, in Eagle Pass, TX.

(Top right) Gov. Holcomb announces Meta will build a data center in Jeffersonville on Jan. 25, 2024.

(Above) Gov. Holcomb meets with members of the Indiana Economic Development Corporation Young Professionals cohort on Jan. 29, 2024, in the Governor's Office.

Gov. Holcomb, with NBA Commissioner Adam Silver at an NBA cares event at Christamore House during NBA All-Star Weekend in Indianapolis on Feb. 15, 2024.

Gov. Holcomb tries an IndyCar simulator at "The Crossover" fan experience on Feb. 16, 2024, during NBA All-Star Weekend in Indianapolis.

Gov. Holcomb talks to Indiana 4-H Ambassadors on Feb. 13, 2024, in the Governor's Office.

Gov. Holcomb shakes hands with Hoosier basketball legend Oscar Robertson (The Big O) on Feb. 16, 2024, during NBA All-Star Weekend in Indianapolis.

Gov. Holcomb thanks Indiana Statehouse Chaplain Matt Barnes on Feb. 20, 2024, during the annual prayer breakfast in Indianapolis.

Gov. Holcomb on stage with AgriNovus Indiana President and CEO Mitch Frazier on March 6, 2024, during an agbioscience event at the AMP in Indianapolis.

Director of Communications Lauren Houck, Press Secretary Erin Murphy, Chief of Staff Earl Goode, and Gov. Holcomb on March 13, 2024, prepping for the final day of his last legislative session as governor.

Gov. Holcomb with fourth grader Charlie Miller from Loper Elementary on March 12, 2024, in the Governor's Office.

Gov. Holcomb and INDOT Commissioner Mike Smith with contractors and state employees in front of a beam they signed that will help connect I-69 to I-465 on March 14, 2024, on the south side of Indianapolis.

Gov. Holcomb behind the bar at Whistle Stop in Indianapolis on March 14, 2024, signing a bill into law allowing business owners to host a happy hour.

(Above) Gov. Holcomb walks toward a couple looking for a cat in the ruins of their daughter's house on March 15, 2024, after a tornado ripped through a neighborhood in Winchester.

(Right) Gov. Holcomb on stage with former Gov. Mitch Daniels on March 19, 2024, during the twentieth anniversary celebration of the Sagamore Institute in Indianapolis.

(Far right) Gov. Holcomb gives an office tour to Mary Gardner on March 18, 2024, before Mary received a Sagamore of the Wabash award.

Gov. Holcomb and First Lady Janet Holcomb with Indiana National Guard members on March 28, 2024, during an Indiana National Guard departure ceremony at Camp Atterbury for guardsmen headed to Texas to support Operation Lone Star.

Gov. Holcomb delivers remarks on March 23, 2024, during the seventieth anniversary celebration of the "Milan Miracle" in Milan.

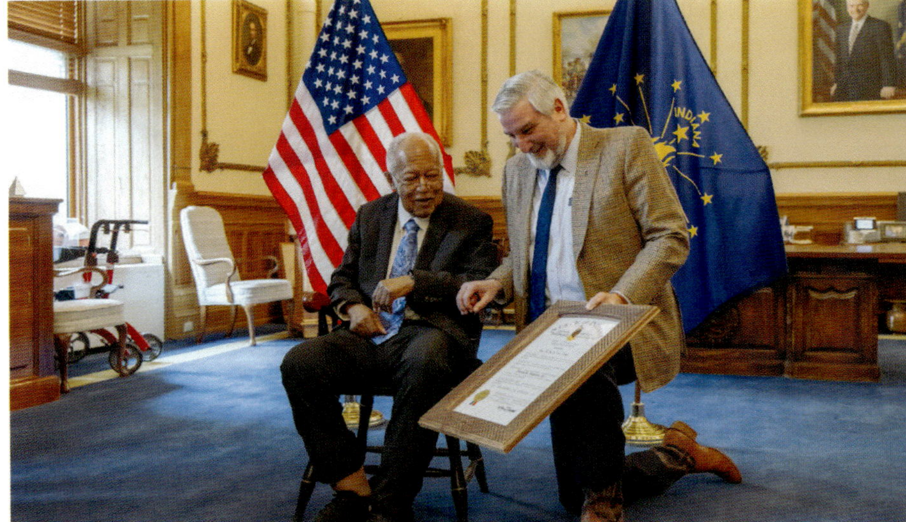

Gov. Holcomb presents a Sagamore of the Wabash award to Andrew Bowman, whose grandfather was a runaway slave who served as a flag bearer in the Union Army during the Civil War. As a result of Mr. Bowman's advocacy and efforts, his grandfather Andrew Jackson Smith was posthumously awarded the Medal of Honor for gallantry under fire during the Battle of Honey Hill. The ceremony was March 27, 2024, in the Governor's Office.

Gov. Holcomb gifts an Indianapolis Motor Speedway flag to SK hynix CEO Noh-Jung Kwak on April 3, 2024, at Purdue University before an announcement that SK hynix will establish an advanced packaging fabrication and R & D facility in West Lafayette.

Gov. Holcomb on a tour of a Heidelberg Materials facility in Mitchell with Heidelberg Materials North America President and CEO Chris Ward and Department of Energy Undersecretary David Crane on March 25, 2024. The group announced that the Department of Energy selected Heidelberg Materials North America as a Carbon Capture Demonstration Project.

Gov. Holcomb presents Consul General in São Paulo David Hodge with a custom Indiana University jersey on April 15, 2024, during an economic development trip to Brazil. Hodge's mother, Jane Woods Hodge, was a former host on WTTV–Channel 4's "Popeye and Janie."

Gov. Holcomb visits "Constitution Grove," where a forest of white oaks are grown for the sole purpose of restoring and refitting the USS *Constitution*, the oldest commissioned vessel still sailing, during a trip to NSA Crane on March 28, 2024.

Gov. Holcomb and First Lady Janet Holcomb hold their Thomas W. Moses Good Scout Awards on April 4, 2024, during the Crossroads of America Council Boy Scouts Character in Action awards dinner in Indianapolis.

Gov. Holcomb applauds as President of Novartis US Victor Bulto cuts the ribbon on a new manufacturing facility on April 4, 2024, in Indianapolis.

Gov. Holcomb and First Lady Janet Holcomb pose for a picture during totality on April 8, 2024, during an event celebrating a total solar eclipse at the Indianapolis Motor Speedway.

Gov. Holcomb claps with NASA Deputy Administrator Pam Melroy and Purdue University President Mung Chiang after kissing the yard of bricks on April 8, 2024, during an event celebrating a total solar eclipse at the Indianapolis Motor Speedway.

Gov. Holcomb and INDOT Commissioner Mike Smith pose with the latest round of Community Crossings Matching Grant winners on April 10, 2024, in Brazil.

Gov. Holcomb speaks on April 26, 2024, during a groundbreaking ceremony celebrating Google's new data center in Fort Wayne.

Gov. Holcomb walks through the Terre Haute Casino on April 10, 2024, during a tour of the facility.

Gov. Holcomb delivers remarks while visiting an Atarraya facility on April 17, 2024, during an economic development trip to Mexico.

Gov. Holcomb and Ambassador of Jordan to the US Dina Kawar Smile inside an Indy 500 pace car on April 25, 2024, after a meeting at the Governor's Residence.

(Above) Gov. Holcomb, Department of Natural Resources Director Dan Bortner, and others cut the ribbon to open the one hundredth mile of trails in the Next Level Trails program on April 30, 2024, in Merrillville.

(Right) Gov. Holcomb, Department of Natural Resources Director Dan Bortner, and Great Lakes St. Lawrence Governors and Premiers Program Director Micheal Piskur plant the ceremonial one millionth tree on the Statehouse lawn on April 26, 2024.

(Above) Gov. Holcomb pumps his fist after cutting a ribbon while surrounded by local, state, and federal officials on May 13, 2024, at a celebration marking the opening of the South Shore Line Double Track project in Gary.

(Far left) Gov. Holcomb gives a thumbs-up to a convention attendee on May 14, 2024, during the opening day of the Sweet and Snacks Expo in the Indianapolis Convention Center.

(Left) Gov. Holcomb holds up a jar of Indiana Dunes National Park Sand on April 30, 2024, during the Northwest Indiana Business and Industry Hall of Fame Lunch in Merrillville.

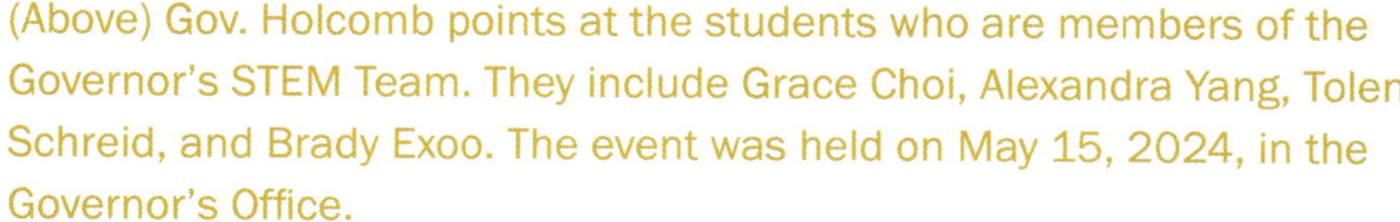

(Above) Gov. Holcomb points at the students who are members of the Governor's STEM Team. They include Grace Choi, Alexandra Yang, Tolen Schreid, and Brady Exoo. The event was held on May 15, 2024, in the Governor's Office.

(Top right) Gov. Holcomb greets Ukrainian Ambassador to the United States Oksana Markarova on May 23, 2024, during the Global Economic Summit in Indianapolis.

(Bottom right) Gov. Holcomb on stage with Eli Lilly CEO Dave Ricks and Senior VP and Director of McGuireWoods Consulting Chris Lloyd on May 24, 2024, during the Global Economic Summit in Indianapolis.

(Top left) Gov. Holcomb does an interview with the IndyCar Radio Network on May 26, 2024, before the Indy 500.

(Bottom left) Gov. Holcomb with European Union External Action Service Deputy Secretary General for Economic and Global Issues Belén Martinez Carbonell on June 4, 2024, during an economic development trip to Belgium.

(Bottom right) Gov. Holcomb celebrates the Governor's Cup victory by the Miss Madison boat, driven by Andrew Tate, on July 7, 2024, during the Madison Regatta on the Ohio River.

(Top) Gov. Holcomb and First Lady Janet Holcomb at the Sydney Harbour in Australia on July 23, 2024.

(Bottom) Gov. Holcomb and Singapore Minister for Foreign Affairs Vivian Balakrishnan on July 29, 2024, during an economic development trip.

(Right) Gov. Holcomb takes a video of a flyover on May 26, 2024, at the Indy 500.

Gov. Holcomb and Zhytomyr Gov. Vitaliy Bunechko shake hands, celebrating a memorandum of understanding while Ukraine President Volodymyr Zelenskyy looks on, on Sept. 5, 2024, in Kyiv, Ukraine.

Lt. Scott Pratt

Trp. Cliff Brooks

Trp. Jim Cruse

Trp. Andrew Forgey

Trp. Aaron Gaul

Trp. Aaron Haney

Trp. Kyle Herron

Trp. Rick Love

Trp. Jerrod Patty

Trp. Josh Tarrh

Trp. Marcus Tow

Trp. Chris Clancy

Sgt. Jim Dungan

STAFF

Margaret Antsy
Courtney Arango
Maggie Ban
Paula Barnett
Liza Bartlett
Amy Beard
Andre Bennin
Ashley Bishop
Clayton Black
Hannah Bond
Luke Bosso
Kathryn Box
Laura Brown
Matt Butler
Abriana Carnes
McKinney Caroline
Cyndi Carrasco
Emily Clancy
Pamela Conway
Stephen Cox
Chris Creighton
Rick Davenport
Steven Donahoe
Jason Dudich
Rachael Ehlich
Olivia Elkin
Isabel Elliott
Joe Elsener
Josie Fasoldt
Sarah Faulkner
Marissa Flick
Maggie Foley
Andrew Forrester
Sam Frain
Pam Fritz
Tim George
Katie Gilson
Jodi Golden
Earl Goode
Alec Gray
Kelsey Green
Hannah Gregory
John Hammond
Joe Heerans
Karrah Herring
Elizabeth Hetler
Rachel Hoffmeyer
Debbie Hohlt
Michele Holtkamp
Rebecca Holwerda
Lauren Houck
Roger Howard
Coni Hudson
Doug Huntsinger
Sam Hyer
Sharon Jackson
Zac Jackson
Christian James
Jane Jankowski
Michael Jefferies
Katie Jenner
Cris Johnston
Kristen Kane
Caitlin King
Lee Ann Kwiatkowski
Sophie Langfitt
Ethan Lawson
Meredith Lizza
Danny Lopez
Adarsh Mantravadi
Linnea Martin
Rachel Massey
Benjamin May
Justin McAdam
James McClelland
PJ Mcgrew
Caroline McKinney
Jessica Mehrlich
Manny Mendez
Jerod Mershimer
Avery Meyer
Daniel Miller
Marianne Molony
Isaac Murdock
Erin Murphy
Katie Murphy
Tyler Ness
Michael Nossett
Jake Oakman
Sam Orrell
Paul Peaper
Anthony Phillips
Joseph Pinnell
Kendra Price
Patrick Price
Chad Ranney
Katie Reed
Bonnie Reed
Olivia Rivera
John Roeder
Veronica Schilb
Kevin Sears
Liza Sherman
Taylor Shockey
Hamilton Smith
Preslie Staggs
Nicholas Stamatkin
Nick Stamatkin
Cora Steinmetz
Susana Suarez
Jim Suess
Shelby Thomas
Colin Thompson
Emma Thorp
Tyler Warman
Stefan Welsh
Joselyne Whipple
Greg Wilson
Stephanie Wilson
Lee Ann Kwiatkowski
Abby Crump
Allison Karns
Micah Vincent

CABINET MEMBERS

Tracy Barnes
Elaine Bedel
Dan Bortner
Matt Brown
Doug Carter
Whitney Ertel
Karrah Herring
Joe Hoage
Rebecca Holwerda
Doug Huntsinger
Joe Habig
Katie Jenner
Cris Johnston
Don Lamb
Chris Lowery
Dale Lyles
Eric Miller
Richard Paulk
Christina Reagle
Brian Rockensuess
David Rosenberg
Ann Lathrop
Daniel Rusyniak
Mike Smith
Joel Thacker
Lindsay Weaver
Suzanne Crouch
Anne Valentine
Kristina Box
Rob Carter
Lesley Crane
Bruce Kettler
Peter Lacy
Teresa Lubbers
Joe McGuinness
Blair Milo
Fred Payne
Bruno Pigott
Jim Schellinger
Terry Stigdon
Jennifer Sullivan

INDEX OF NAMES

ABOUT THE AUTHOR

Eric J. Holcomb, Indiana's 51st governor, is a lifelong Hoosier who served in the US Navy at home and abroad. During his two terms as governor, Indiana achieved historic economic growth through cutting taxes and reducing state debt. Holcomb spearheaded major infrastructure projects, including historic roads, trails, broadband, and new housing programs. His education and workforce initiatives boosted teacher salaries, expanded job training, and aligned education with industry needs. He led a transformation of Indiana's public health system, increasing funding by 1,500 percent for local health departments. Committed to community development, Holcomb invested in parks, conservation, and renewable energy. A champion of public safety, he modernized law enforcement and appointed an unprecedented 120 new judges. Holcomb served on two national governors' executive committees during his tenure. He and his wife, Janet, reside just outside of Indianapolis.

Special thanks to Alec Gray and Stefan Welsh for so many of the photos; Mindy Colbert for her work putting this volume together; and all those who supported the publication of this book.